LOOKIN' for LIGHT

Science Adventures with Manny the Origami Moth

by Eric Braun

illustrated by Jamey Christoph

A young girl made the final fold on her origami moth. "I will name you Manny," she said. Then she ran outside to join her friends.

Manny looked around. Where were *his* friends? He tested his paper wings. Slowly he lifted into the air and flew out the window.

Manny blinked in the bright light. "Where is all that light coming from?" he wondered out loud.

A bee that was flying nearby heard Manny.

"That bright ball in the sky is the sun. It's the biggest source of light and warmth in the world. Without it Earth would be dark and cold."

"I like the dark."

"Most moths do, but plants and animals **need** **sunlight** to survive. Plants use sunlight to make their own food. Without sunlight, plants would die. Then animals that eat plants would die too. Soon all living things would disappear."

"Wow, life without the sun would be **scary.**"

"Don't worry. The sun will keep shining for billions of years," said the bee.

"Where are all the **moths**? I would like to meet some moth friends."

"I don't meet too many moths. They're active at night. I'm busy mostly during the day."

6

"It's daytime now, but it's darker here by these plants. Why is that?"

"Shadows. These plants block light because they're opaque. That means light can't go through them. Light hits a leaf and stops. A shadow is created behind the leaf, where the light can't go."

"Light can go through some things. Glass and water, for example, are transparent. Look at the girl's legs in that pool."

"I can see her legs in the water, but they seem to bend."

"Yes, light goes through transparent things. But the light slows down and bends when it goes through the transparent object. The bending of light is called refraction. When light is refracted, it changes the way we see things," said the bee.

"I'll say!" said Manny.

Eyeglasses have lenses. Transparent materials like glass or plastic can be used to make lenses. Lenses are specially shaped to curve light inward or outward. They help people see things better.

"I can see a little bit of light coming through that kite. Is it **transparent?**"

"It is **translucent.** That means it allows some light through, but not all."

The two friends were quiet for a few minutes as they watched the sun setting behind the buildings.

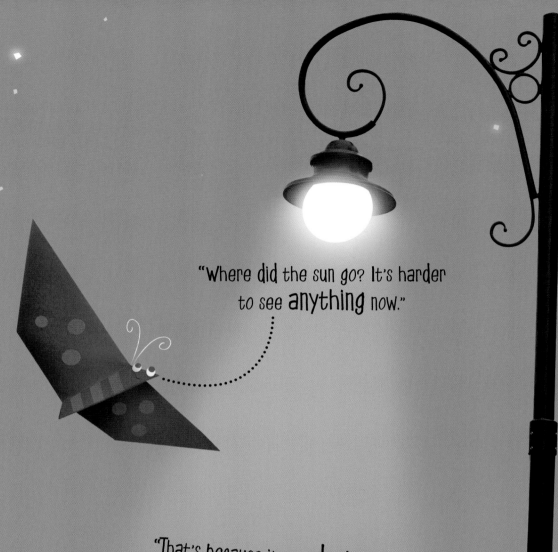

"Where did the sun go? It's harder to see **anything** now."

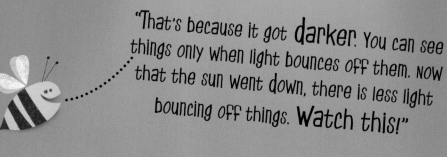

"That's because it got **darker**. You can see things only when light bounces off them. NOW that the sun went down, there is less light bouncing off things. **Watch this!**"

MORE LIGHT BOUNCING OFF AN OBJECT MAKES IT EASIER TO SEE.

LESS LIGHT BOUNCING OFF AN OBJECT MAKES IT HARDER TO SEE.

The bee yawned.

"I have to go to bed. **Good night.**"

He buzzed away, and Manny was alone.

"I wish I could find some moth friends. I would look in these trees and bushes, but it's really dark. The lamplight shines straight down and does not bend toward the trees."

Light travels in a straight line called a ray.
It can't bend around corners very easily.

Manny saw some floating lights near the pool.

"Hey! Glowing bugs! Are you moths?"

"No. We're **fireflies**. We make our own light inside our bodies."

"I can see your light in the water." Manny said. "That's cool!"

Light can change direction by bouncing off smooth surfaces such as mirrors and still water. The bouncing of light is called reflection.

"Do you want to see something else that's cool?" asked one of the fireflies. "Come look at these flowers in the light."

"What beautiful colors!"

"Did you know that **all** the colors are contained in light? When light hits an object, some colors are **reflected**, and some are **absorbed**. The color an object reflects is the color we see. We can't see the colors that are absorbed."

"So this red flower reflects **only red light**. But the lamplight that's hitting it has **all** the colors?"

"Right," said the firefly. "The flower reflects red and absorbs the other colors."

If all the colors in the rainbow are absorbed when light hits an object, we see the object as black. If all the colors are reflected, then we see the objects as white.

Manny said good-bye to the fireflies and started toward home. He had not found any moth friends, and he was disappointed. But then he spotted something.

"Hey, up there! Are you moths?"

"Hi, paper moth," one of the moths said.

"Hi, real moths! I thought moths like darkness. Why are you by that light?"

"We love darkness! But people have some really cool lights. This one reminds us of the moon."

"I see what you mean," Manny said.

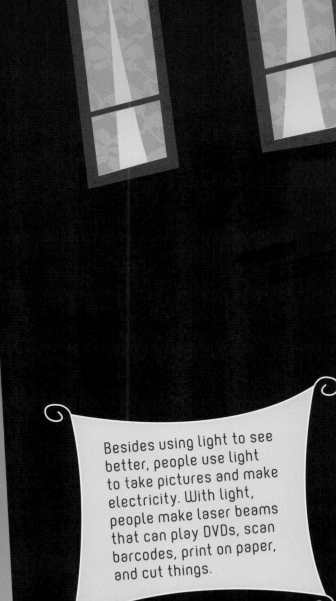

Besides using light to see better, people use light to take pictures and make electricity. With light, people make laser beams that can play DVDs, scan barcodes, print on paper, and cut things.

Just then, Manny heard a noise from the window. "I better get home," he said. "I'll come back to see you guys tomorrow night!"

Manny zipped through the window just when the girl and her friends were coming into the room to make more paper moths.

"There you are, Manny!"

At one day old, Manny was a wise old moth. Tomorrow he would take his new paper moth friends outside to learn all about light.

20

GLOSSARY

absorb—to soak up

laser—a thin, high-energy beam of light

lens—a piece of curved glass or plastic in a pair of eyeglasses; also the clear part of the eye that focuses light

opaque—blocking light

ray—a beam of light; it travels in a straight line unless it is reflected or refracted by an object

reflection—the returning of light from an object; also, when an image of something shows on a shiny surface like water or a mirror

refraction—the bending of light as it travels through something that is transparent or translucent; often, refracted light can change the way objects appear

translucent—letting some light through, but not all

transparent—letting all light through

READ MORE

Jacobson, Ryan. *Step-by-Step Experiments with Light and Vision.* Mankato, Minn.: Child's World, Inc., 2012.

Shaffer, Jody Jensen. *Vampires and Light.* Monster Science. Mankato, Minn.: Capstone Press, 2013.

Silverman, Buffy. *Me and My Shadow: A Book About Light.* My Science Library. Vero Beach, Fla.: Rourke Pub., 2012.

MAKE AN ORIGAMI MOTH

Manny is one bright moth! Check out these instructions to make your own origami moth.

what You need

origami paper

WHAT YOU DO

FOLDS

Valley folds are shown with a dashed line. One side of the paper is folded against the other like a book. A sharp fold is made by running your finger along the fold line.

Mountain folds are shown with a white dashed and dotted line. The paper should be folded sharply behind the model.

Arrows

single-pointed arrow: Fold the paper in the direction of the arrow.

half-pointed arrow: Fold the paper behind.

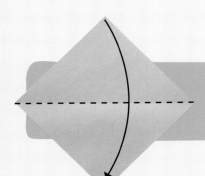

1. Start with the colored side down. Valley fold the paper in half.

2. Valley fold past the top edge.

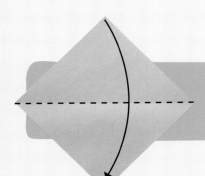

3. Mountain fold in half.

4. Valley fold the top layer to the left.

5. Mountain fold the right side.

6. Lift up the two wings.

7. Your moth is finished!

INDEX

colors, 16, 17

Earth, 4

lasers, 19

lenses, 8

opaqueness, 7

plants, 5, 7

rays, 13

reflection, 15, 17

refraction, 8

shadows, 7

sun, 4, 9, 10

sunlight, 4, 5

translucency, 9

transparency, 8, 9

INTERNET SITES

FactHound offers a safe, fun way to find Internet sites related to this book. All of the sites on FactHound have been researched by our staff.

Here's all you do:

Visit *www.facthound.com*

Type in this code: 9781479521869

Super-cool stuff! Check out projects, games and lots more at
www.capstonekids.com

more books in the series:

Diggin' Dirt: Science Adventures with Kitanai the Origami Dog

Glowing with Electricity: Science Adventures with Glenda the Origami Firefly

Lookin' for Light: Science Adventures with Manny the Origami Moth

Simply Sound: Science Adventures with Jasper the Origami Bat

Thanks to our advisers for their expertise, research, and advice:
Paul Ohmann, PhD, Associate Professor and Chair of Physics
University of St. Thomas

Terry Flaherty, PhD, Professor of English
Minnesota State University, Mankato

Editor: Shelly Lyons
Designer: Ashlee Suker
Art Director: Nathan Gassman
Production Specialist: Danielle Ceminsky
The illustrations in this book were created digitally.

Picture Window Books are published by Capstone,
1710 Roe Crest Drive, North Mankato, Minnesota 56003
www.capstonepub.com

Library of Congress Cataloging-in-Publication Data
Braun, Eric, 1971-
Lookin' for light : science adventures with Manny the origami
moth / by Eric Braun.
pages cm. — (Nonfiction picture books. Origami
science adventures)
Summary: "Engaging text and colorful illustrations and photos
teach readers about light"— Provided by publisher.
Audience: 4-8.
Audience: Grade K to 3.
Includes bibliographical references and index.
ISBN 978-1-4795-2186-9 (library binding)
ISBN 978-1-4795-2943-8 (paperback)
ISBN 978-1-4795-3322-0 (ebook pdf)
1. Light—Juvenile literature. 2. Moths—Juvenile literature.
3. Origami—Juvenile literature. I. Title. II. Title: Looking for light.
QC360.B715 2014
535—dc23
2013032480

Photo credits:
Digital illustrations include royalty-free images from Shutterstock.

Capstone Studio: TJ Thoraldson Digital Photography 22-23;
Shutterstock: benokky1972, 9 (top left), Dmitry Kosterev, 7
(bottom), Richard Griffin (flowers), 16, 17, Volodymyr Burdiak
(pool), 8, 14-15, Webspark, 8 (bottom)

Printed in the United States of America in Stevens Point, Wisconsin.
092013   007768WZS14